ILLUSTRATIONS WITH BLACK BACKROUND

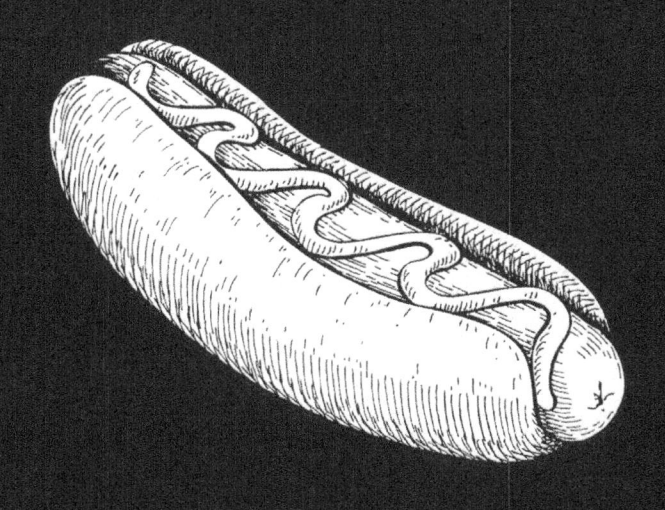

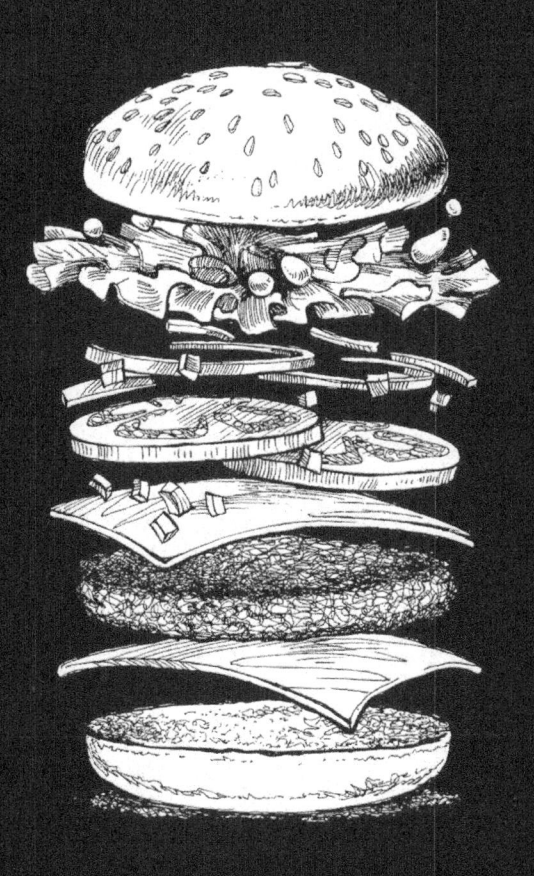

SNACK

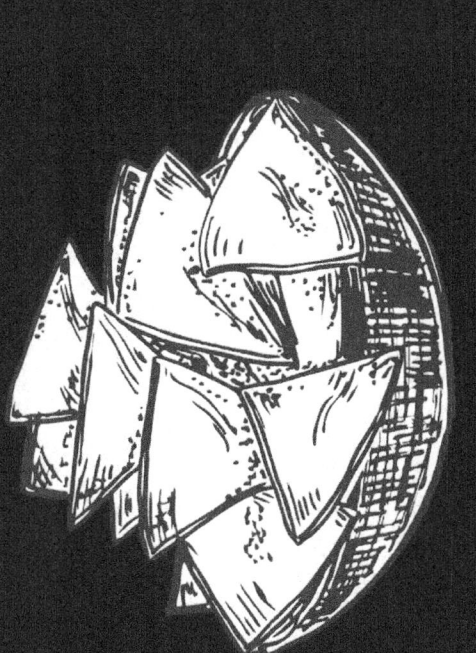

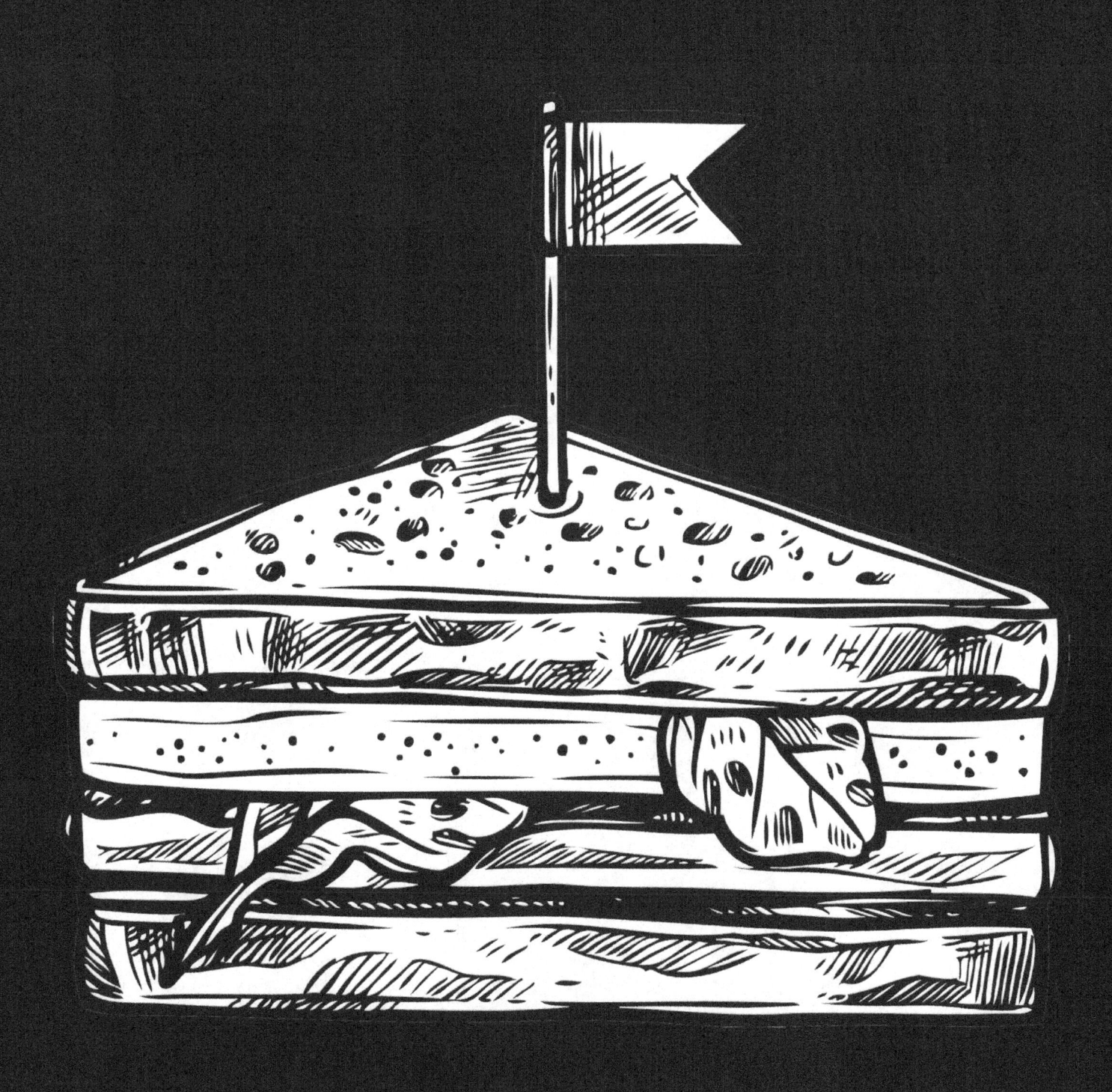

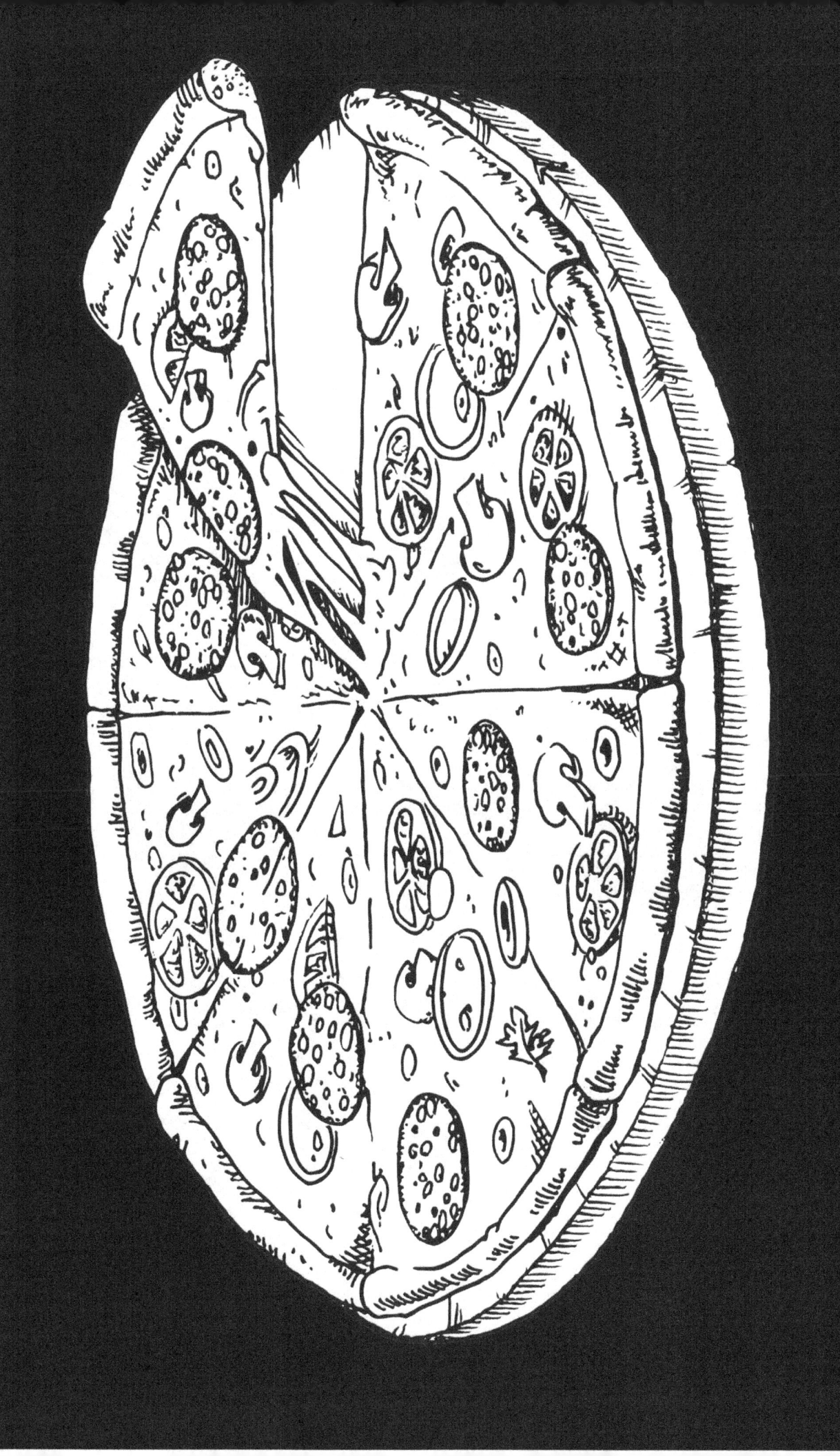

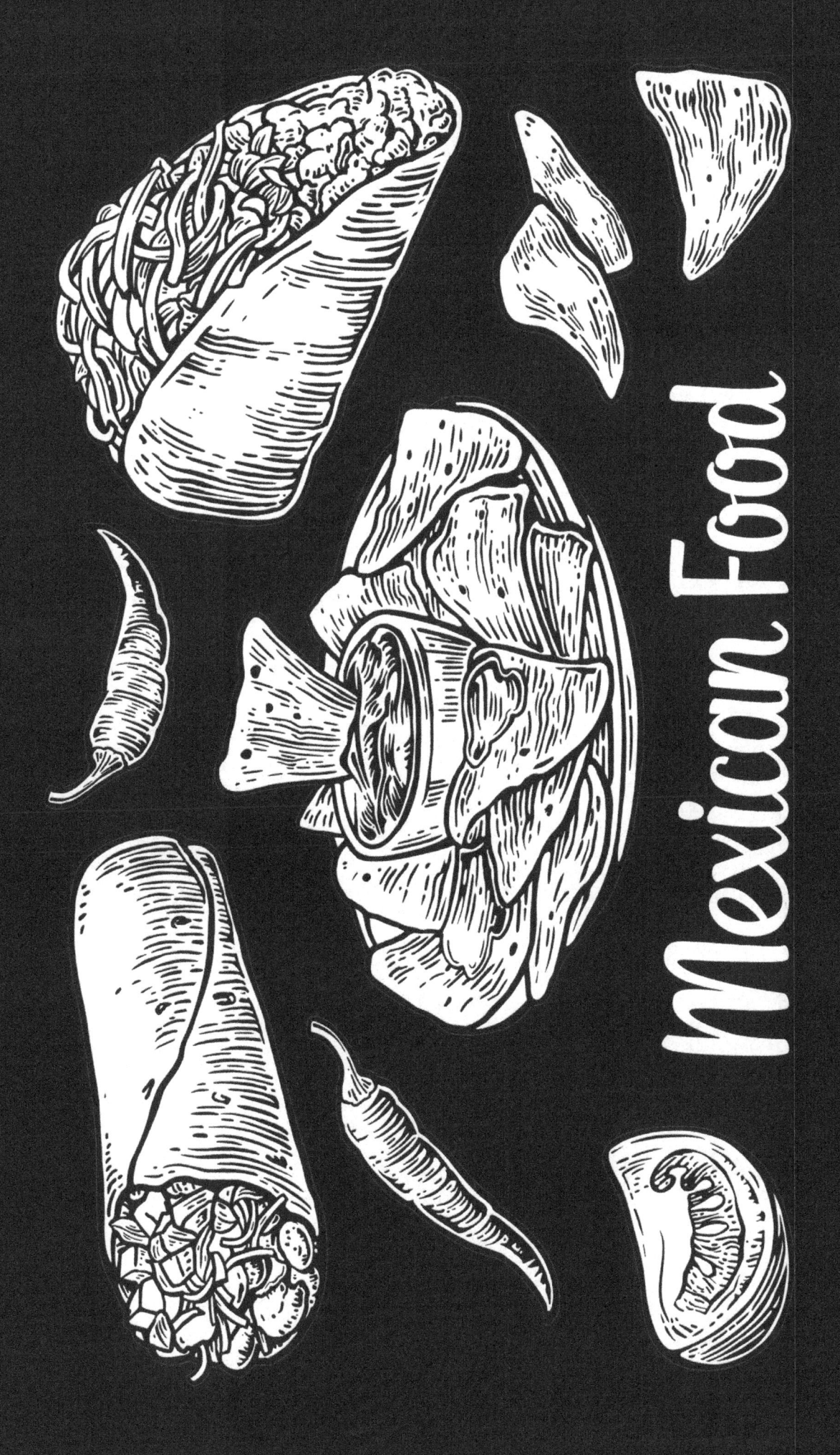

Mexican Food

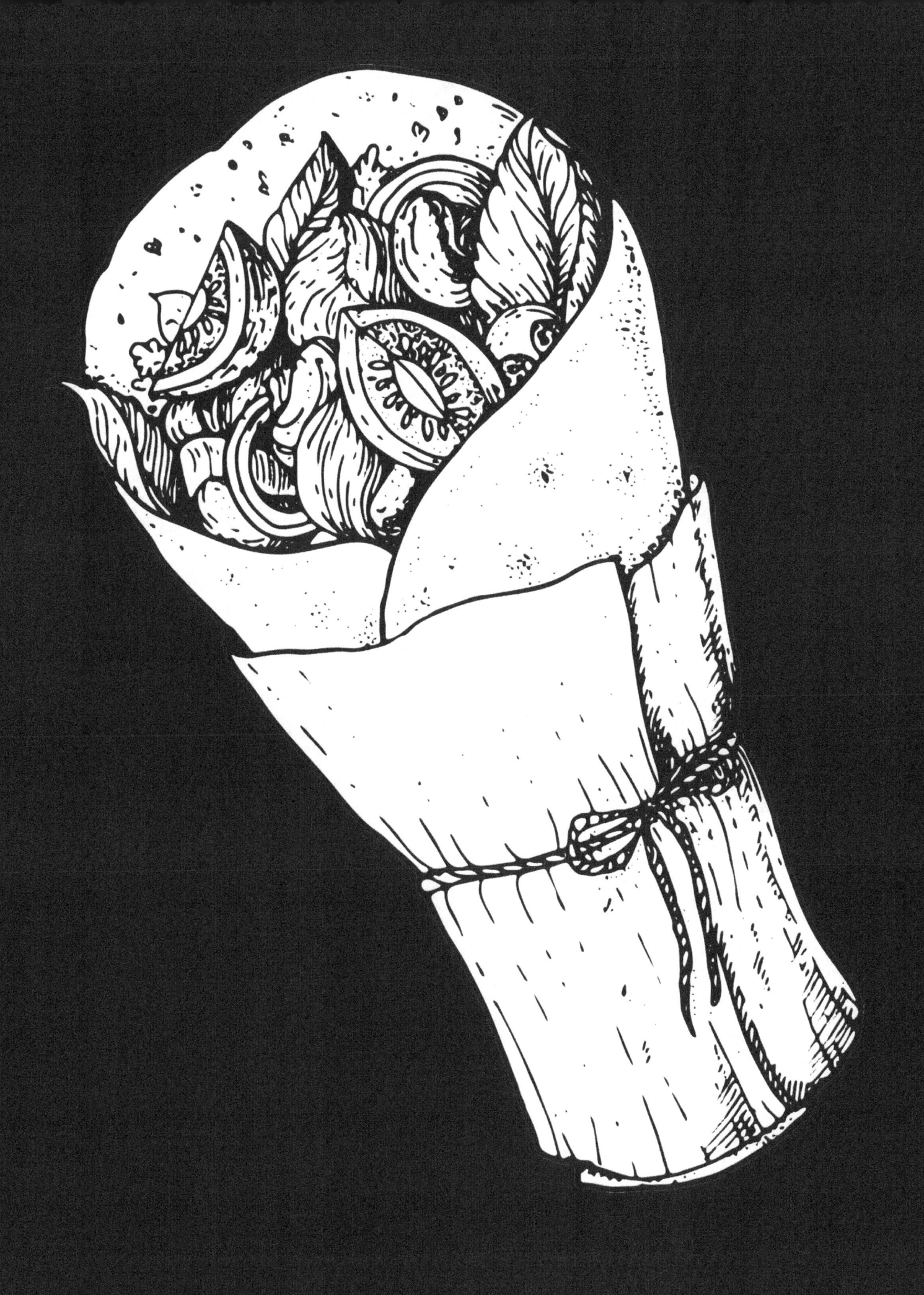

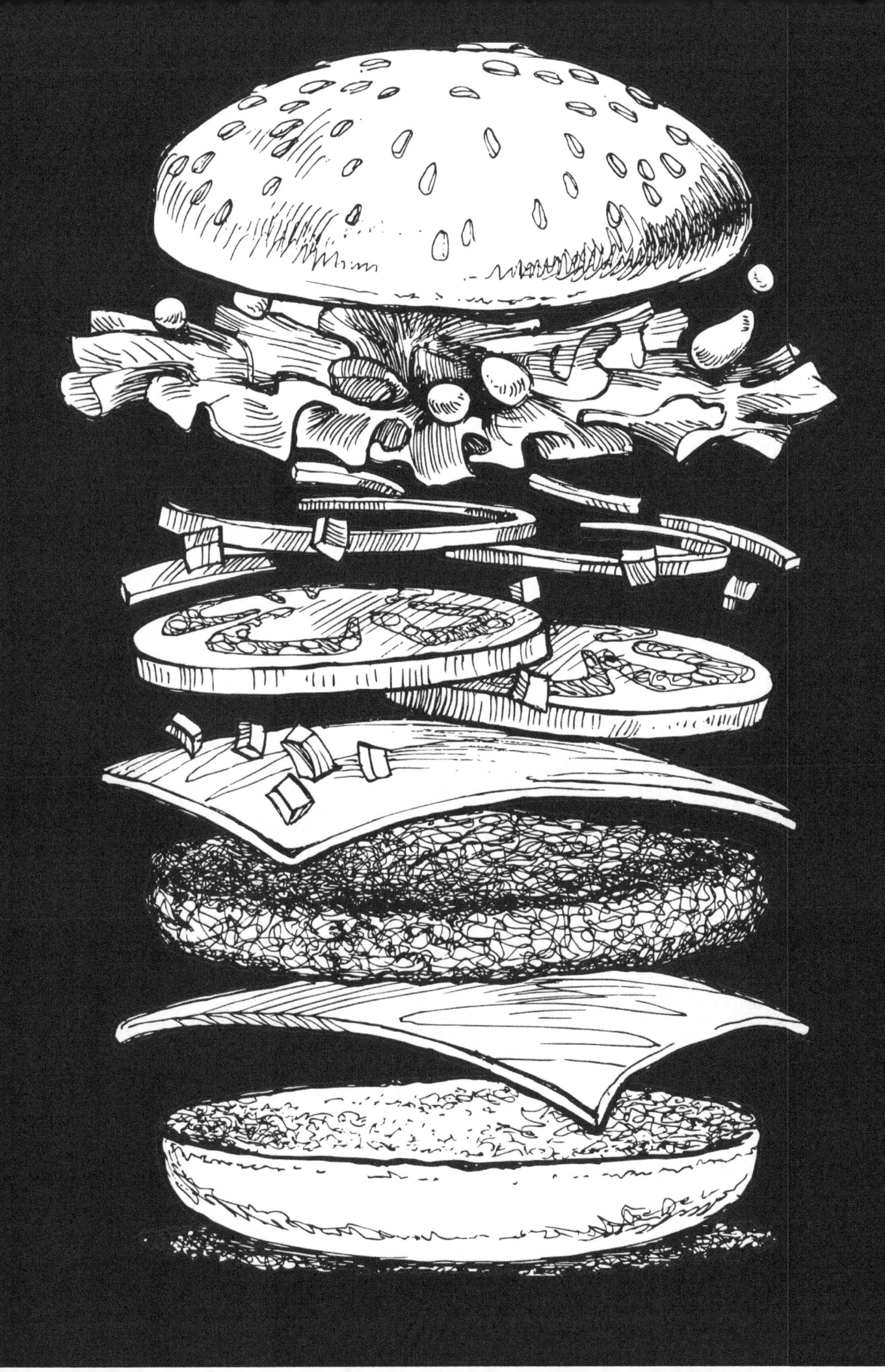

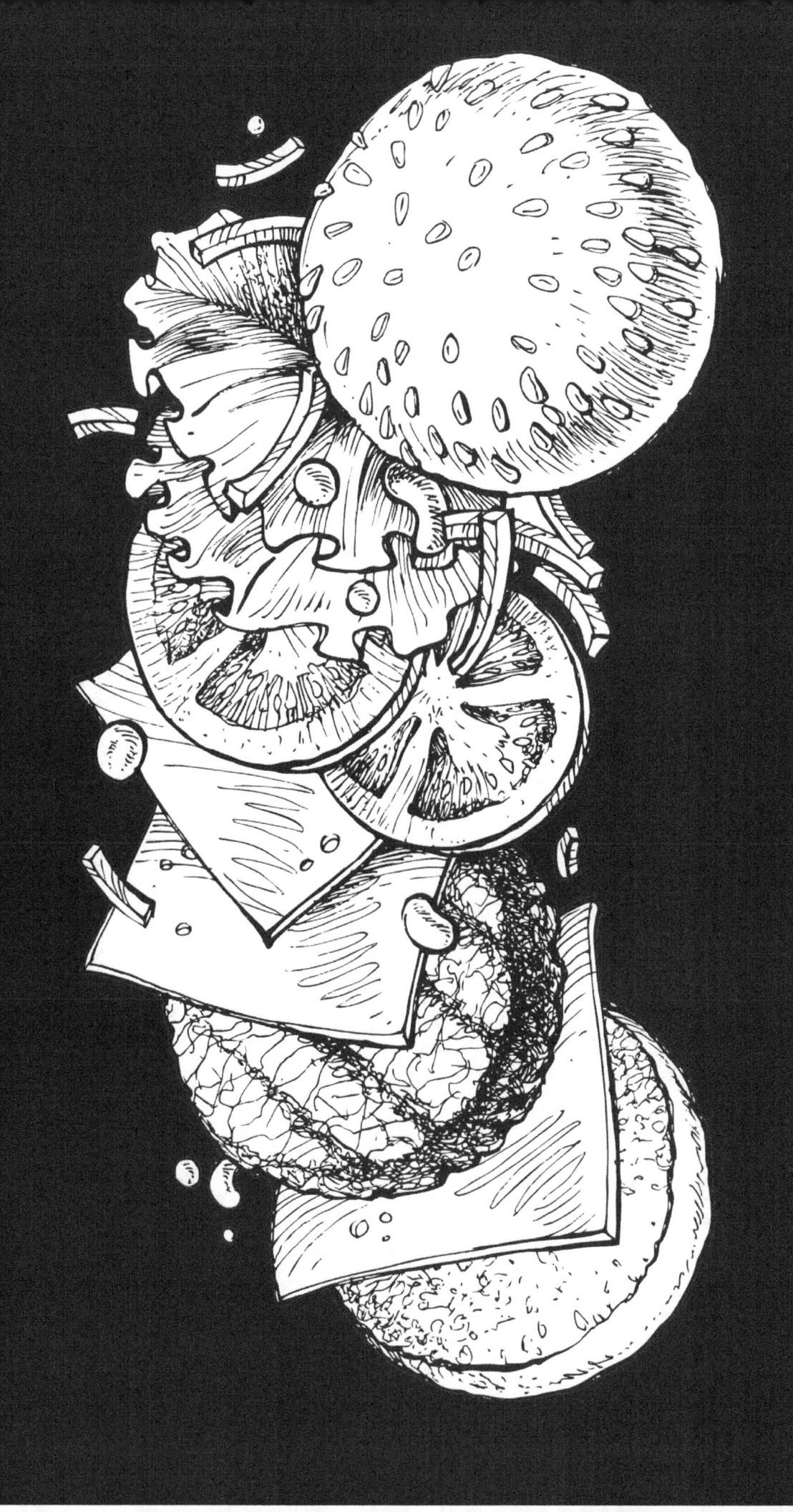

ILLUSTRATIONS WITH BLACK BACKROUND

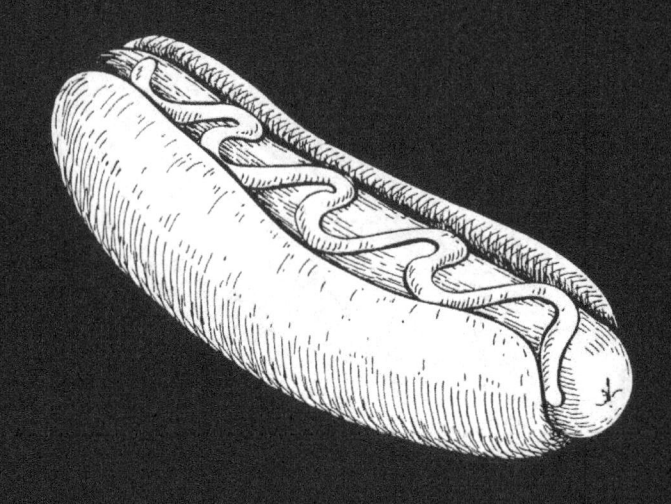

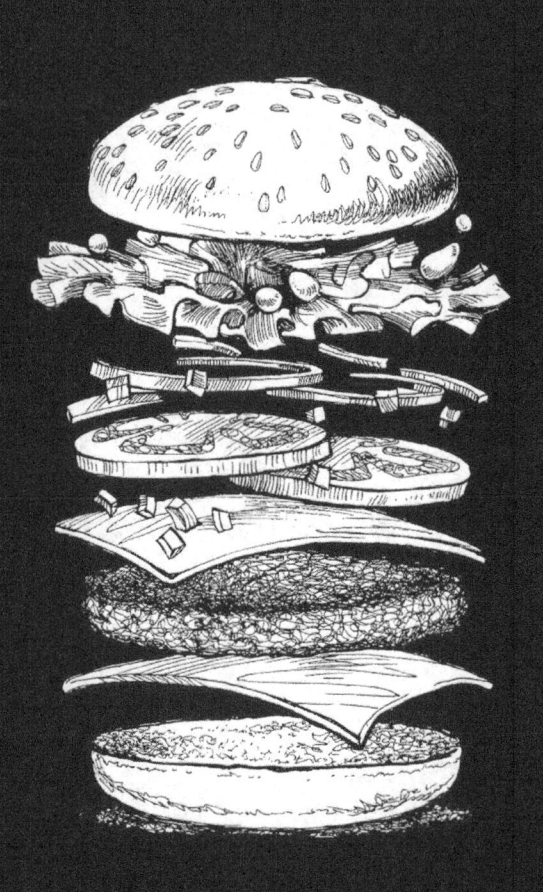

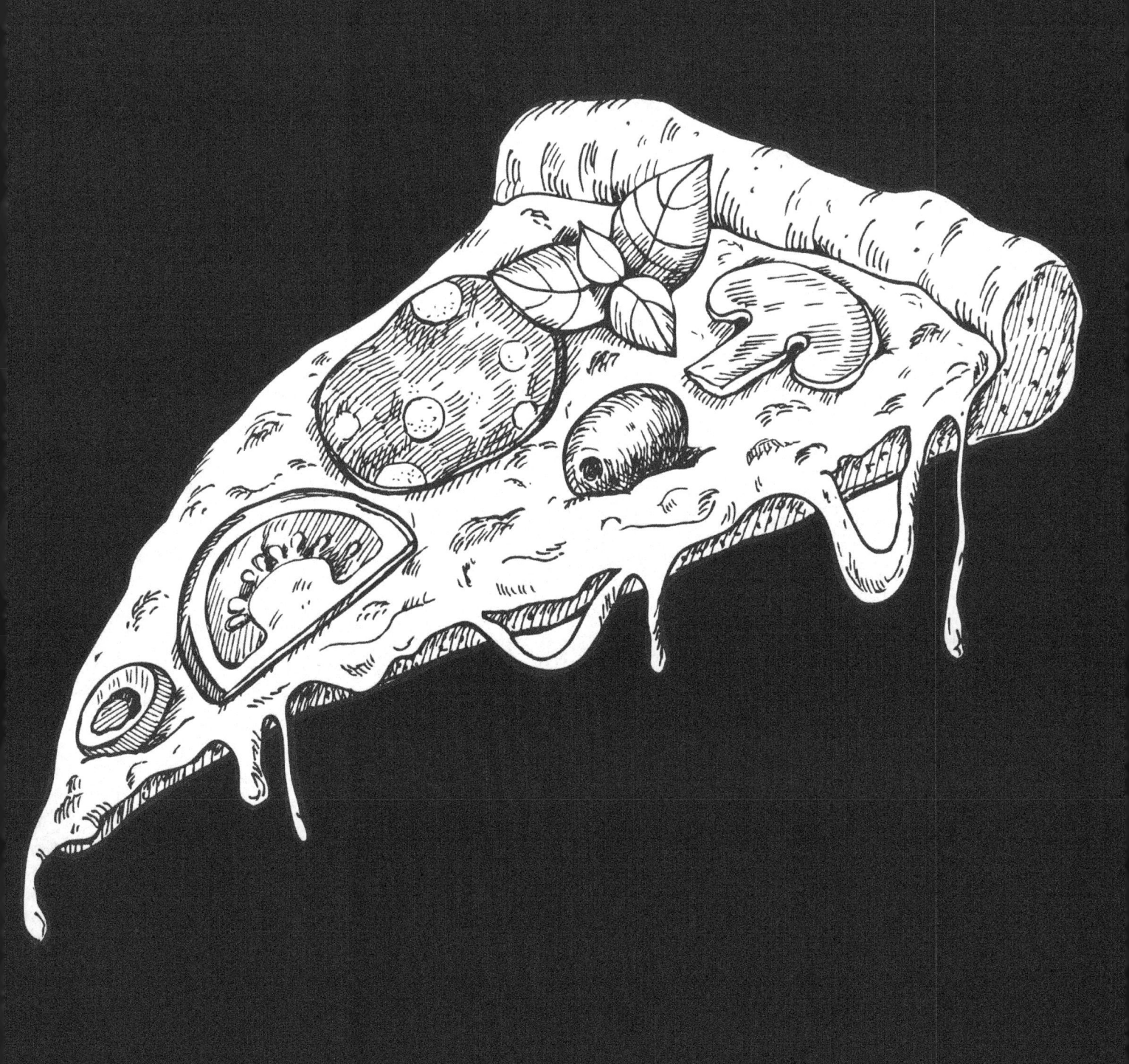

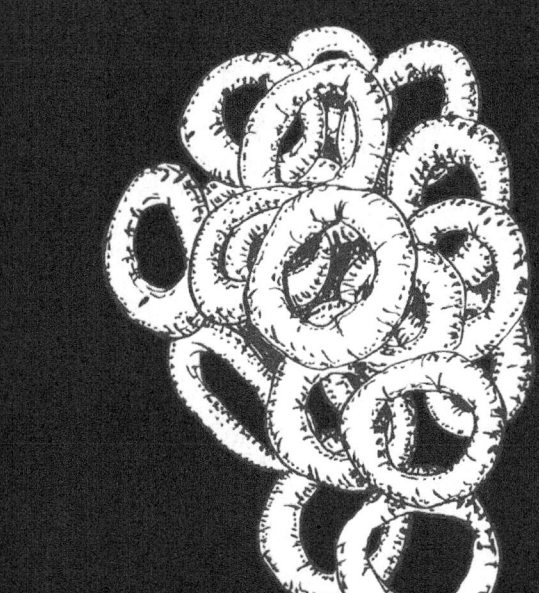

SNACK

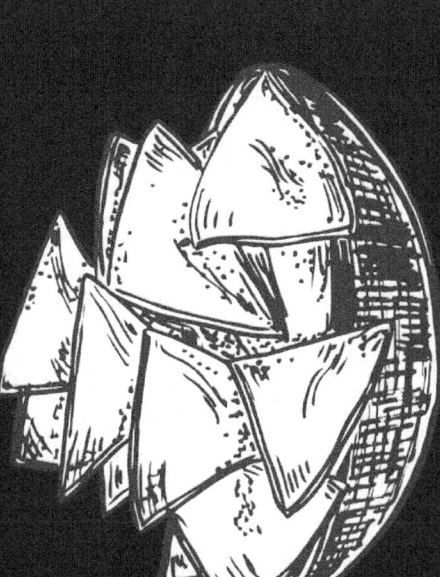

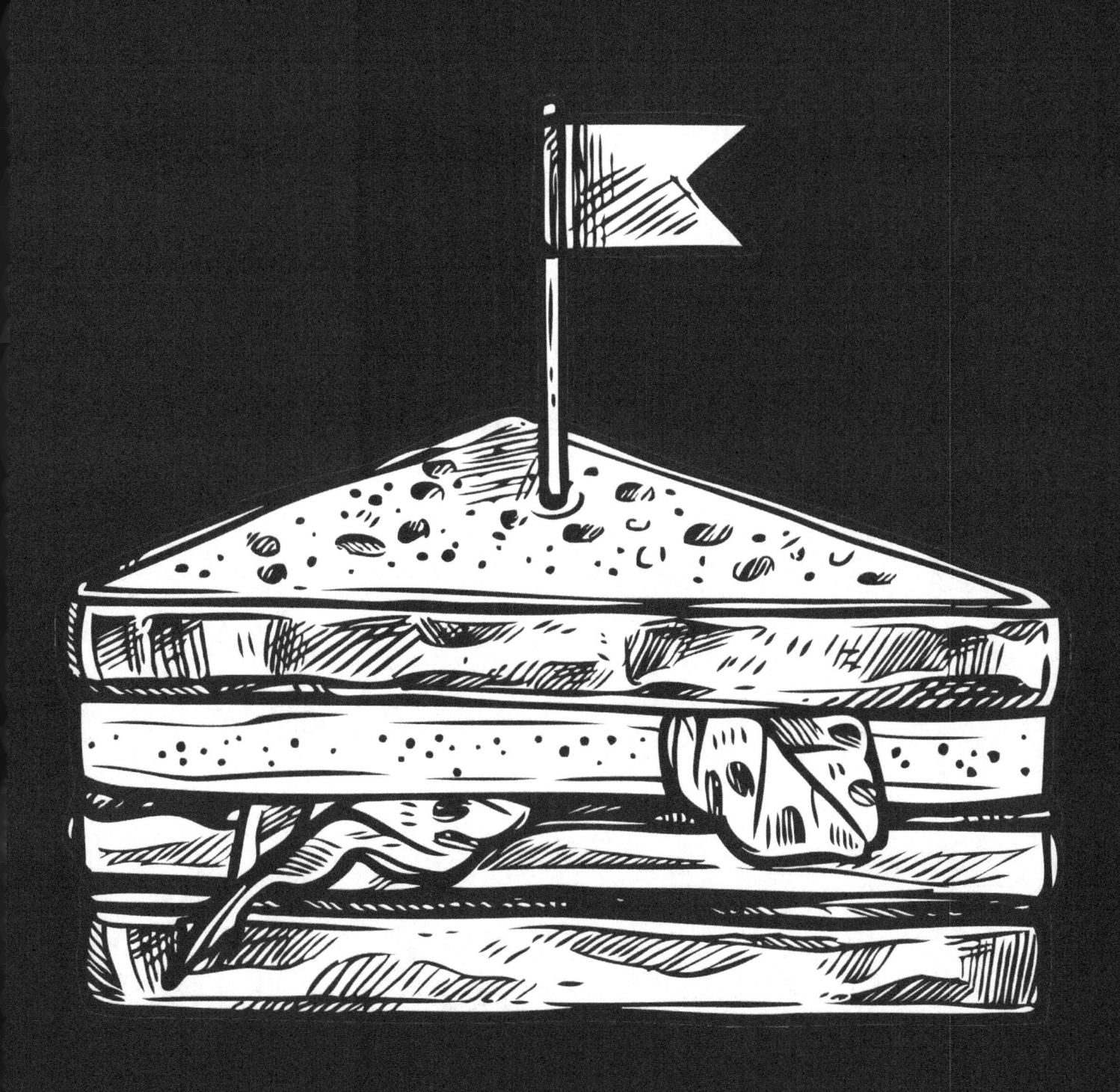

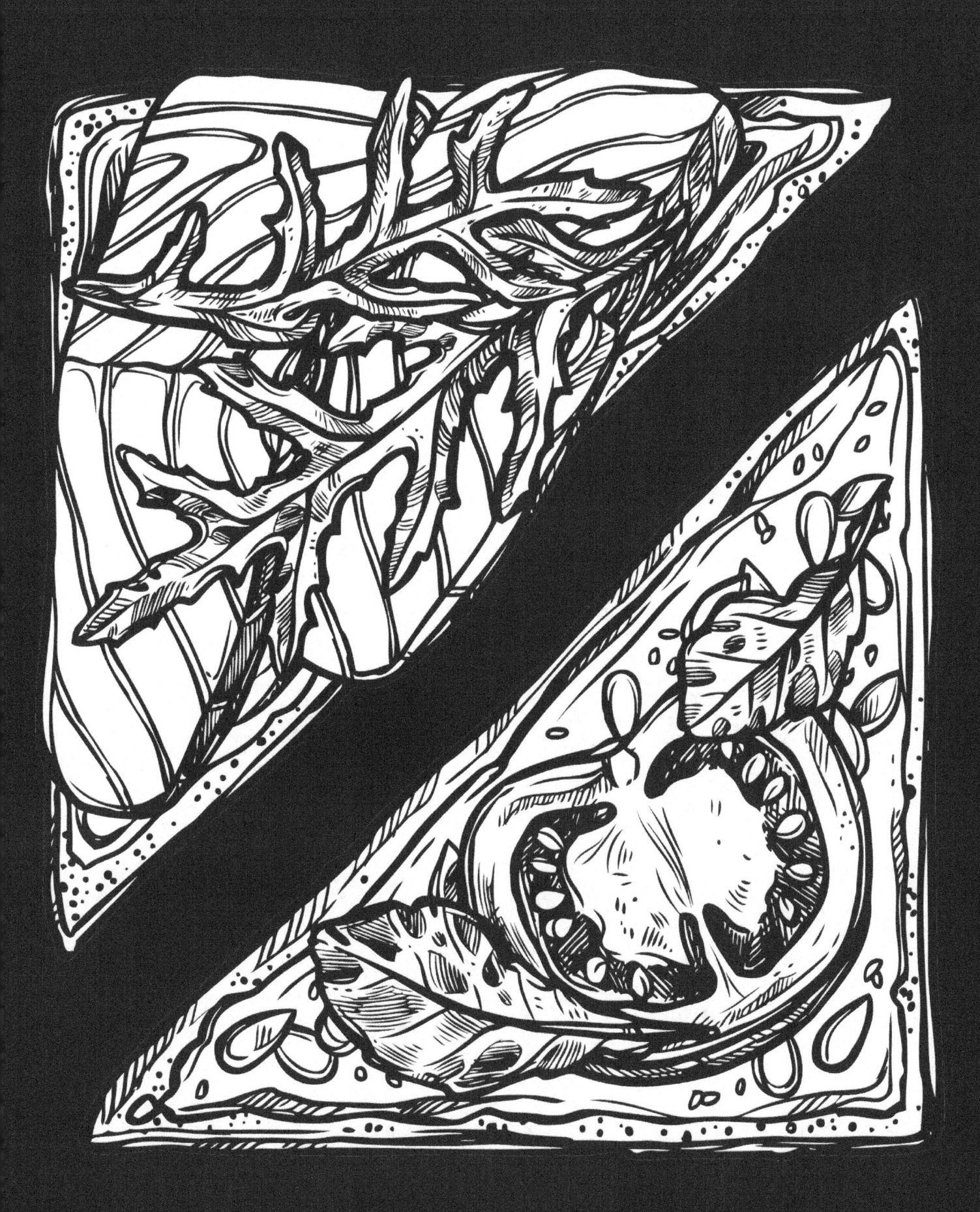

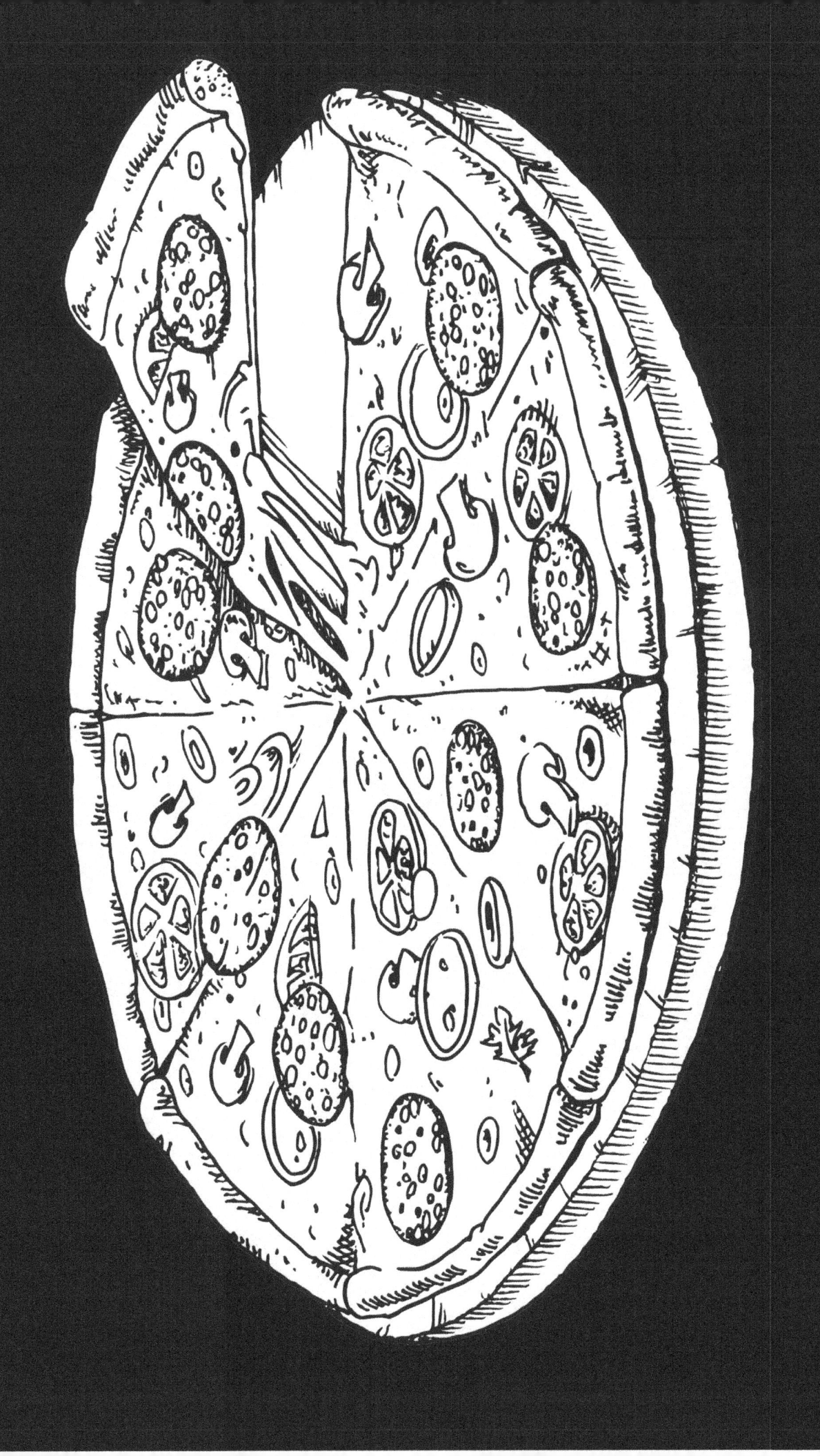

Mexican Food

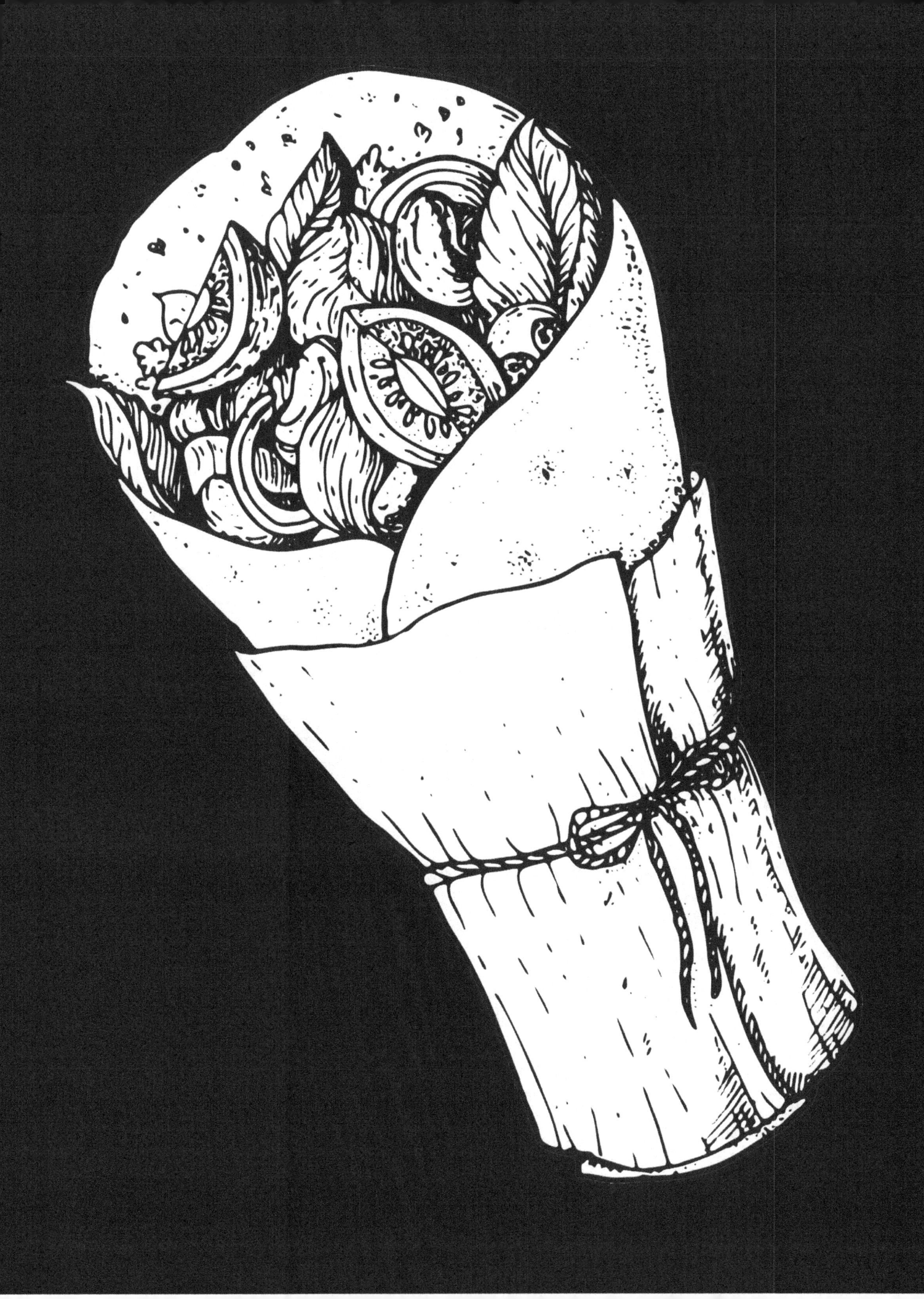

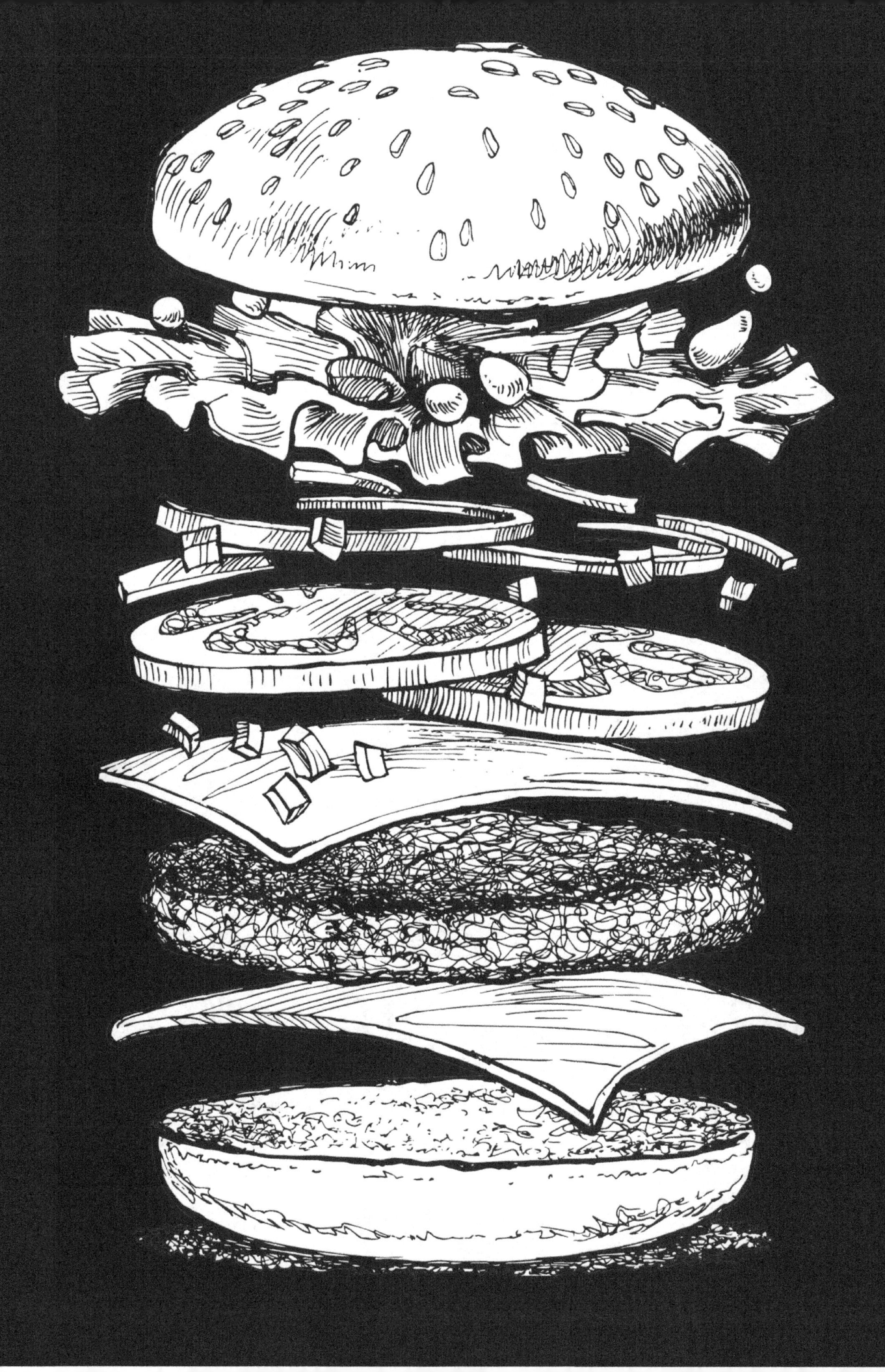

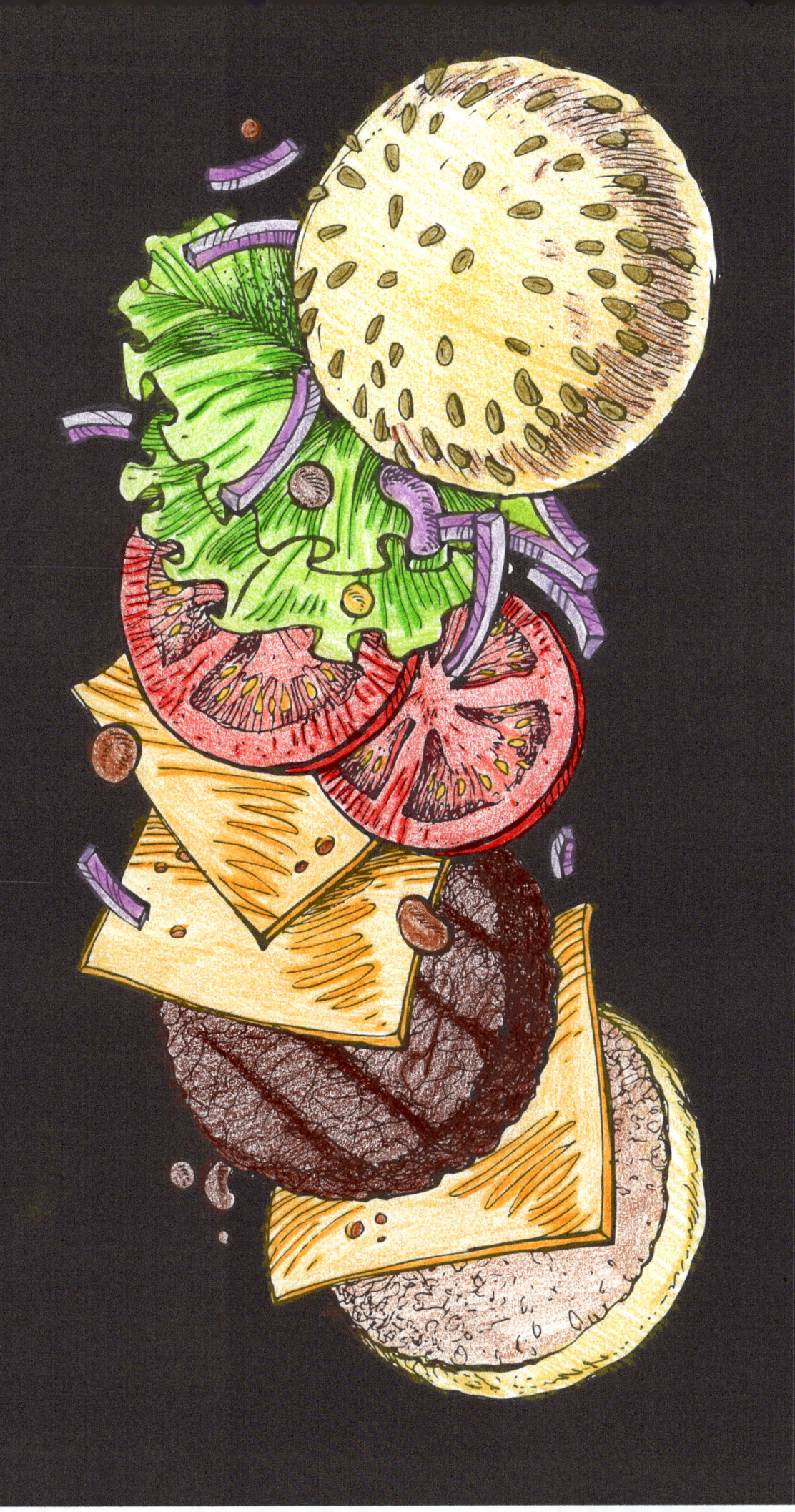

IMPRINT:
published 2019 by Marcel Dornis
Geratalstraße 4, 99094 Erfurt
E-Mail: triberion90@gmail.com

Made in the USA
Coppell, TX
27 March 2020